Pack It Up

A Book for the Contemporary Traveler

Special thanks to the passengers, tour members and travelers who have contributed many of these invaluable travel tips.

Dedicated to my father whose sea stories enticed me to travel to the four corners of the world-to experience my own—

And my mum, who continually packed my suitcases to ensure that I made it in one piece.

Your purchase of this book benefits CARE, the world's largest international relief agency. To find out more about CARE, please call 1-800-521-CARE

Cover Photo by Conrad & Company Photography
Cover Design by Kelly Vance
Text Illustrations by Lee Vance

ISBN 0-9627263-0-3
Library of Congress 90-082758

For more information, contact:
Flying Cloud Publishing
PO Box 16057
Seattle, WA 98116-4057
(800)-977-PACK

Manufactured in the United States of America

Contents

·1·
Before You Go

Three important steps to a successful trip:
1. Read
2. Ask
3. Plan

Read anything you can get your hands on about your destination, from the travel section in the Sunday newspaper to guidebooks. Before you rush out and spend money budgeted for your trip on lengthy books, check out the library, which has a wealth of information on travel and almost all destinations in the world. Find out which guides fit your needs specifically before you buy them.

Ask family, friends, and travel agents questions about your destination. People love to share their experiences and their knowledge. How often have we all received invaluable information through a casual conversation? Your reading should prompt many questions and now is the time to find the answers.

Plan ahead. Advance planning can save you money and help alleviate stress further down the road. By planning and asking, you may receive many discounts that you were unaware existed, from prebooking savings to off-season and senior discounts. The following are a few suggestions before you go:

- Look into educational tours related to your profession. They could be tax-deductible and save you money.

- Research tour companies. Specialized tours, such as sports tours, are a great way to meet people with the same interests and save money.

- Travel agencies are free- many people do not realize the amount of time and money they can save you. With the new computerization, it takes only minutes to find the least expensive airfare to any destination. Call and compare prices for all your travel needs. Just like types of luggage, different agencies have different features and prices. There is nothing more valuable than a good travel agent.

- Ask your travel agent for promotional videos, maps or tour books.

- Most importantly, ask your travel agent or a friend to teach you how to read an airline ticket if you are not familiar with one. It's all too common for travelers to be left stranded, because they didn't know how to double check the departure date or time on their ticket.

- Always reconfirm your domestic airline ticket 24 hours in advance and your international ticket 72 hours in advance.

- Check your local video store for videos about your destination. They don't have to be travel guides specifically. For example, you may see feature or fictional films about the Amazon that include authentic native customs, history, and scenery.

- If you have time, call the 800 numbers for the airlines listed in your telephone book and see what, if any, special flights they may have available.

- Check all your travel documents! Make sure the airline you fly is the same one listed on your ticket jacket. This is a problem many travelers run into *after* they are dropped off at the airline terminal.

- Write the Chamber of Commerce or National Tourist Office for additional information on your destination. Ask specifically for maps, dates of events, or whatever you are interested in. Addresses can be obtained at local libraries or the telephone book.

- Borrow some language learning tapes from your local library. Learn a few key phrases before you need them. If you're really serious about learning a foreign language, check college extension courses, or buy tapes and take them and a small cassette recorder with you.

- Obtain or renew your International Driver's License.

- Have a full medical and dental check-up.

- Research to find out if special precautions (such as inoculations, malaria pills) are needed for your destination.

· 2 ·

Luggage Tips

The most important luggage tip is to check out your luggage long before your holiday to assure that all cases are in working order. Second to you, they will be the most important thing to survive your trip. Most travelers find out the hard way that the first three letters in the word *"luggage"* spell *"lug"*.

Examine the hinges, wheels, seams, straps, zippers, and especially handles for wear and tear. Most luggage stores and shoemakers can make any necessary repairs.

If you are in the market for new luggage, take into consideration what type of travel you will be doing overall. Ask friends and family what their favorite piece of luggage is and why. And before you purchase your luggage, be sure to lift and carry it or roll it around the store once or twice to see if it's manageable. (If possible, see how it rolls onto an escalator for ease in airports and hotels).

Luggage Dimensions

Carry-On: Your carry on must fit under your seat or in the overhead compartment. The maximum weight allowance for a carry-on bag is 40 pounds, but a maximum weight of 20 pounds for ease in handling is suggested. You may also carry on such personal items as a purse (not so large as to be considered another carry-on), camera, coat, and umbrella. Again, check with your specific carrier for their allowances as they vary depending on plane structure.

Checked Luggage-Domestic: The maximum is two pieces of luggage per traveler, with a maximum weight allowance of 70 pounds per piece. The luggage may not exceed 62 inches in total dimensions (each bag), which is height, width, and length combined. This is subject to variability of the carrier.

Checked Luggage-International: The same as checked luggage on domestic flights, but check with the airline for specific luggage allowances for your flight. Generally, international flights are more restrictive than domestic.

Excess Baggage: If you are traveling for an extended period of time and feel that it is necessary to bring more luggage than allowed, consider sending it to your destination via air freight instead of checking it. It can be very expensive to fly with excess baggage, and cumbersome as well!

Following are hints and ideas to assist you with your luggage once you have it:

- Never put your home address on your luggage! This is a sure way of telling everyone that you are not at home, in case you arrive at your destination and your bag is circling the baggage terminal in another airport. It is not mandatory in all airports to show your baggage claim check upon entering or exiting the baggage terminal, and anyone may have access to your luggage and home address on the tag.

- Instead, put your travel agent's address and telephone number, a relative, a trusted neighbor, or your office/work number. Of course, leave a detailed copy of your itinerary including hotel addresses with someone you trust. It wouldn't do any good for airport personnel to call your home anyway, as there wouldn't be anyone there to answer!

- Always place an ID tag on your carry on bag as well.

- Place a copy of your ID and itinerary inside your luggage in full view, in case you are separated from it. This way it stands a chance to catch up with you. Also, tags often are torn off along the way due to frequent handling.

- Constantly count your luggage while traveling (including carry-ons, briefcases and purses) to assure that something was not left on the plane, train, bus, taxi, or ship.

- Before leaving home: Take a photo of your luggage (including carry-ons). This photo will serve as a reference in case your luggage is lost and assist with baggage and insurance claims. Quite often travelers are very flustered (understandably) when their luggage is misplaced and forget what they actually brought. Traveling frequently and bringing different cases on various trips can add to the confusion.

- Remove all old baggage claim tickets from your bags. They are easily confused when traveling, so keep them at home in your scrap book. Remember to remove all carry straps from your luggage before checking it on the plane. They tend to catch on other objects and are quite often damaged or missing when you receive your luggage at the other end.

- To help keep your luggage looking new, place luggage in inexpensive machine washable luggage covers.

- Do not buy cheap luggage. The mental anguish is not worth the savings. However, designer luggage will be stolen before old, worn luggage every time, so consider your luggage purchases seriously. Paying extra for designer labels may not be worth it in the long run. A middle-of-the-road luggage purchase is usually the safest bet.

- The serious shopper should check into expandable suitcases. They can be found in a variety of sizes and styles. Generally, they are soft-sided bags with zippers at the top and bottom. Be sure to check the wheels and the carry straps to assure the bag is strong enough to get it all home.

- For major shopping holidays, pack a small suitcase with all your items, then place it inside a large empty suitcase. When you are ready to return home, fill the empty one with your purchases.

- Always lock your luggage, not only to discourage theft, but to add extra strength in keeping it closed. Purchase small, inexpensive locks to keep the outside pockets of bags closed en route.

- Carry extra keys to your luggage. Combination lock luggage has an advantage over key locks, since you don't have to risk searching for lost keys. As most luggage keys will open luggage of a similar type, ask the hotel or your neighbor for a key if you do forget or lose yours.

- Use a luggage strap around the girth of your suitcases to keep them securely closed. Be sure to write your name on it in ink to discourage people from taking it along your travel route.

- A lightweight nylon zip bag with shoulder strap for any extra purchases made along the way packs easily. How often have we all needlessly spent money on another bag when our closets are full of them!

- Don't put your title on your luggage tag, for example, Dr., Capt., Prof., etc. This increases your chance for theft.

- Make an old fashioned "pom-pom" in a bright color yarn to tie on the handle of your luggage. This makes it more personalized and easier for you to identify on the baggage carousel and in large groups of bags.

- Spray a large "dot" in the center of your case, using a fluorescent color, and no one will want it!

- Use brightly colored surgical or electrical tape in a unique design or your initials to identify your case and as a deterrent to thieves.

- Put your initials in the upper right-hand corner of your luggage for added identification. Inexpensive stencils can be purchased at a department store; when so many bags look alike, this will help you identify yours.

Tips on Storing Luggage

- Place crumpled-up newspapers inside luggage to help keep dampness and mildew to a minimum. The paper will absorb the wetness. Change every few months.

- If dampness occurs in luggage, use a hairdryer to eliminate it. Also to cut down on dampness, cut a deodorant bar of soap in half and place inside your luggage during storage.

- Cedar shavings or kitty litter are also suggested for stored luggage.

- Place a few dryer sheets (Bounce, Downy) inside each bag. This keeps them smelling fresh and clean.

- If your luggage has been stored for quite awhile, place it open in the sunshine to air it out before packing.

- To clean your luggage: Use a small hand vacuum cleaner or whisk to clean the inside of your cases. The small size allows you to get into the corners.

- Remove stains from luggage fabric immediately with soap and water to avoid odor later when damp. When you return home, the bag can be professionally cleaned at either a dry cleaner's or luggage shop. Check the manufacturer's label prior to using any cleaning solution. Water-repellent sprays work wonders on soft-sided luggage to prevent stains and keep water from soaking in.

- Spend part of a lazy afternoon finding which keys belong to which suitcases. Once you have them together, use twist ties from the kitchen to secure them to the proper handle. (A fun game with children and grandchildren!) Safety pin the keys inside the suitcases when not in use.

- Do not check your luggage curbside unless it is absolutely necessary. It is best to take it inside to the counter. The ticket counter has up-to-the last minute information of your flight details in case of cancellation or delay.

Luggage Insurance There are various ways to insure luggage; check with your travel agent first and find out how much your luggage is insured by your airline or the tour company you are traveling with. If you are traveling on your own, or are interested in additional luggage insurance, here are some options:

- Inquire into your homeowner's coverage, which generally covers your personal belongings up to an amount stated in your policy, including cameras and luggage.

- Ask your travel agent to recommend a travel insurance policy. They usually have a few to choose from, with varying amounts of coverage at varying fees.

- If you charge your air, tour or cruise tickets with certain major credit cards, you automatically may be covered, at no extra charge, against loss or significant damage to your baggage when traveling with a large carrier company (plane, bus, train, or ship). Confirm your card benefits, as they are subject to change.

· 3 ·

Planning Your Travel Wardrobe

Choosing a travel wardrobe of basics will help you deal
with space limitations. Build your wardrobe using
one or two basic colors, so the same shoes, hosiery and
accessories can be worn with everything. Some
versatile color combinations are black and red, navy and
red, brown and beige or black and white.

Simple, classic styles for dress and casual wear usually
work best. Make sure that each item of clothing
can be worn at least two ways.

For warmer climates, pack lighter colors and natural
fabrics, such as cotton. Unlike synthetics, cotton
breathes. For cooler climates, dark colored clothing which
can be layered for warmth is a good choice.
Wool gabardine is a good fabric to travel with as it's
lightweight, warm and wrinkle resistant.

One tip that many travelers forget is that you are wearing
an entire day's outfit as well as all the clothes that you have
packed. For plane travel, loose-fitting clothing with elastic
waistbands and comfortable shoes for walking long
distances in airports is suggested.

Organizing your wardrobe is easier if you have a list of
things that you plan to take with you. Keep the list of items
in your carry-on bag. If checked bags are misplaced, the
list of contents can help identify them.

Women's Weekend Travel Wardrobe

_ 1 pair of pants
_ 1 skirt
_ 1 jacket to match pants and skirt
_ Shorts (if appropriate)
_ 2 Knit T-Shirts
_ Evening blouse
_ Lightweight raincoat
_ Swimsuit (if appropriate)
_ Pareo
_ 1 pair low heeled pumps
_ 1 pair walking shoes
_ Sandals (if appropriate)
_ Nightgown
_ 2 belts (one in each basic color)
_ Jewelry
_ Lingerie
_ Hosiery
_ Scarf
_ Small handbag
_ Umbrella (if appropriate)
_ Athletic wear (if appropriate)

For a six to twelve day trip, add these items:

_ Second pair of shorts
_ Second pair of pants
_ Cardigan sweater (cotton or wool)
_ Additional scarves
_ Solid colored dress
_ Second swimsuit (if appropriate)
_ Additional lingerie and hosiery
   (depending on often you plan to launder)

For a three-week trip, add these items to both the aforementioned groups:

- Skirt w/matching top
- Third pair of pants/walking shorts
- Additional T-Shirts
- Tank Top
- Additional lingerie and hosiery
- Second nightgown

Men's Weekend Travel Wardrobe

- 1 pair of casual slacks
  (the color khaki goes with almost anything)
- 1 pair of dress slacks
- 1 jacket which coordinates with both slacks
- Tie (if appropriate)
- 2 short sleeved shirts (1 polo and 1 T-shirt)
- 1 long sleeved shirt
- 1 sweater
- Shorts
- Swimtrunks
- 2 belts
- Undershorts
- Undershirts
- Casual socks
- Sleepwear
- 1 pair casual shoes
- 1 pair thongs or sandals
- 1 pair dress shoes (if appropriate)
- Lightweight overcoat
- Umbrella (if appropriate)
- Athletic wear (if appropriate)

For a six to twelve day trip, add these items:

- A suit (dark for formal occasions)
- V-neck or crew neck sweater with coordinating slacks
- Additional pair of shorts
- Additional undershorts and undershirts
- Additional socks

For a three-week trip, add these items to both the aforementioned groups:

- 1 pair casual pants
- Sweatpants- neutral color
- Sweatshirt-neutral color
- Additional tie
- Additional underclothing
- Additional shirts

Children's Weekend Travel Wardrobe

- 2-3 T-Shirts
- 1-2 pair leggings
- Swimsuit
- 1 large T-shirt (for pajamas or cover-up)
- 3-4 underpants
- Long sleeved shirt
- Shorts
- Skirt or pants
- Sweatshirt
- Rainjacket with hood
- Belt
- Socks
- Dress clothes (if appropriate)

- Dress shoes (if appropriate)
- Hat, gloves, boots, sunglasses
- Sneakers
- Sandals or thongs

For a six to twelve day trip, add these items:

- Additional sweatshirt
- Additional swimsuit
- 1-long sleeved shirt
- 3 T-Shirts
- 5-7 underpants
- Socks
- Nice sweater
- Pajamas

For a three-week trip, add these items to both the aforementioned groups:

- Additional sweatpants
- Underclothing
- Slippers

• A great idea for packing children's clothing is to put an entire days outfit (including underwear and socks) in a large ziplock freezer bag and write the child's name on the outside of the bag. This helps when traveling with more than one child and saves time searching through luggage for individual items.

·4·

Pack It In

There is such a wide spectrum of travel these days that you need to tailor your packing to fit your travel needs. Packing wisely can save unnecessary problems and expenses. Be sure to pack lightly, and only pack what you can carry for one mile without putting it down!

Always start by making a check list. It will speed up packing and let you know what you might be missing.

Never pack the following items in checked luggage: money, medicine, expensive jewelry, travelers checks, travel documents including your airline ticket, matches, cigarette lighters, butane for curling irons. Ask your travel agent if you are unsure of any other questionable items.

Travelers' Packing Check-List:

Following is a list of basic items to consider taking with you. Some items are, of course, a must; others are optional depending on the destination.

❑   Tickets
❑   Passport
❑   Travelers checks
❑   Cash
❑   Credit card (s) *only those needed*
❑   Local currency
❑   Medication
❑   Itinerary

- ❏ Luggage
- ❏ Address book and pens
- ❏ Photocopies (one for you, one for someone at home) of each of the following:
  - ❏ Passport ID page and Visa pages
  - ❏ Airline tickets
  - ❏ Credit card (s)
  - ❏ Travelers checks
  - ❏ Itinerary
- ❏ Moneybelt
- ❏ Language phrasebook
- ❏ Guidebooks & maps
- ❏ Healthy snacks
- ❏ First aid kit
- ❏ Sewing kit including scissors & tweezers
- ❏ Swimsuit and sunscreen
- ❏ Jewelry, scarves and accessories
- ❏ Reading material, magazines
- ❏ Sunglasses
- ❏ Camera and film
- ❏ Extra passport photos
- ❏ Business cards
- ❏ Travel journal
- ❏ Travel alarm clock
- ❏ Adapters & converters
- ❏ Inexpensive gifts
- ❏ Extra glasses and/or contact lenses
- ❏ Eye glass repair kit
- ❏ Comb, hairbrush
- ❏ Flashlight with batteries
- ❏ Pocket knife
- ❏ Skin moisturizer, lubricating eye-drops, lip balm
- ❏ Small tape recorder
- ❏ Small calculator
- ❏ Toothbrush, paste, floss

- ❏ Deodorant
- ❏ Moist towelettes
- ❏ Only keys needed upon return home
- ❏ Extra plastic bags
- ❏ Eye-covers and ear-plugs
- ❏ Elastic clothesline
- ❏ Extra shoe laces, string
- ❏ Travel clothing (see Chapter 3)
- ❏ Hat
- ❏ Sense of Humor

Packing Your Carry-On Suitcase:

If possible, try to travel with only carry-on luggage. If your carry-on bag is heavy and does not have wheels, you should either borrow one with wheels or consider purchasing one. This saves the muscles in your shoulders and your back.

Pack as many items as possible in your carry-on bag in plastic Ziplock bags. They are easier to identify and when you pull them out, everything else doesn't fall to the bottom.

Most importantly, if you are traveling to a meeting or a special occasion and you must be dressed appropriately, be sure either to wear what you need or carry it on the plane with you. No worries over lost or misplaced luggage.

When in doubt, leave it out!

Interlayering is the name given to the following method of packing either soft-sided or hard-sided luggage and is the most successful in preventing wrinkles in your clothes. Begin with your suitcase open on a flat surface.

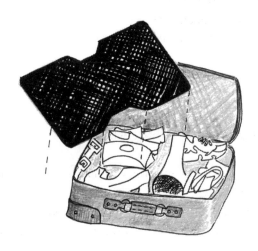

(#1) Place your shoes in pairs with the toe-tucked-in the heel method inside plastic bags. Put your shoes and all heavy items along the bottom of the suitcase (near the hinges). Place belts along the perimeter of the case and heavy items, such as hairdryer, cosmetic case, etc.

Now place a divider on top of these items. If your suitcase does not come with a divider, you can make your own by either: a) folding a plastic dry-cleaner bag into thirds b) using an over-sized placemat or c) cutting a piece of cardboard the size of your suitcase (with cut-outs for your hands to lift it out) and cover it with contact paper.

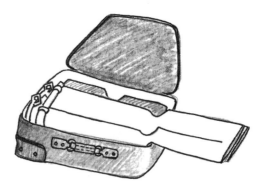

#2 Fold your slacks along their natural creases and place the waistband against one edge of your suitcase with the bottom of the pant extending over the opposite edge of the case. Place the second pair of slacks in the same method in the opposite direction.

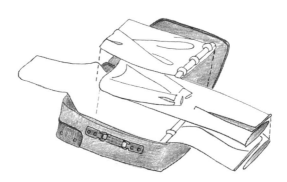

#3 Continue folding your skirts and dresses along their natural creases and use the "Interlayering" technique of layering each article in the opposite direction until all your slacks, skirts, and dresses are packed.

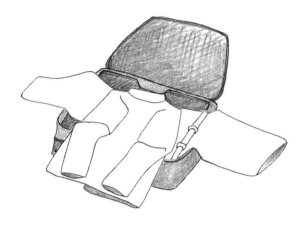

#4. Next, button all jackets/blazers and pull a dry-cleaner bag over them. Place them face down in the suitcase with the sleeves being brought to the back of the jacket along their natural creases. The bottom of the jacket(s) will extend over the top edge of the case.

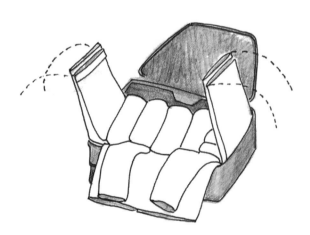

#5. Roll up all knit items and place them on top of the layered clothing, leaving the original articles extended over the edges of the case. When you have utilized every inch of space, bring the ends over the rolled items inside the case, alternating sides as you go. This keeps your clothing in a rounded shape without getting creases in the knee area of the slacks and jacket waistlines. It is also easier to pull out certain items you may need without disturbing the entire case of clothes.

#6 When all items are packed, the benefit of having the divider in the middle of the suitcase is that you can reach in and lift-out the entire top layer of your packed items without disturbing them and retrieve items on the bottom half of the suitcase. (or add items to the bottom half).

Additional Hints For Packing A Suitcase:

- Pack all of your heavy items (hairdryer, shoes, converter) on the bottom of your case. Stuff your shoes with socks, hose, underwear, anything that won't wrinkle easily. Don't forget that you can cover your shoes by pulling a sock over the outside of them.

- An oldie but a goodie: Place tissue paper between folds.

- For packing pleated skirts, turn them inside out, wrap masking tape around the hem (to keep the pleats set), and pull into an old pair of panty hose with the top and bottom cut off. This will keep the pleats in and the skirt from wrinkling. Place around the perimeter of case.

- Roll your outfits together if they are knits. They won't wrinkle and you won't have to search for all your accessories. Add matching socks and underclothes.

- If you are traveling with more than one suitcase, number your suitcases and catalogue your items as you pack.

- Wrap men's ties around a piece of cardboard and secure with a wide piece of elastic.

- Sweaters are easy to roll up, usually don't wrinkle, and fit well into the corners, thus keeping other items from shifting in your suitcase.

- When using dry-cleaner bags, make sure that the bag does not have advertising printed on it. The ink can rub off on clothing.

- Turn all sequin items or embroidered clothes inside out and place in either a plastic bag or pillowcase to minimize rubbing and loosening sequins. (This also allows you to have your own pillowcase on your trip.)

- Use your evening bag to store your jewelry so you know exactly where it is and with which outfit you plan to wear it in case you're in a hurry.

- Stuff all the corners in your luggage with small, soft items to save space: socks, underwear, hose, and all things that won't wrinkle.

- Fold blouses and men's shirts inside out so the wrinkles are facing inside and not so prominent.

- Place items that you intend to use first on the top of your suitcase: shorts, bathing suit, pajamas, etc.

- The contents of a suitcase will settle, leaving more space for additional items if packed the day before departure. Pre-packing allows peace of mind and time to clear out the refrigerator.

- Place men's cufflinks and studs in plastic or felt containers and put in jacket pockets.

Packing Your Garment Bag

There are many different types and sizes of garment bags on the market. Some have built-in frames and some are simply heavy material designed to cover your clothes. Depending on the specific type of garment bag you have, the following suggestions will assist you in packing it more successfully for your next trip.

When packing your garment bag, use a maximum number of three hangers. Begin by placing your garment bag on a flat surface. Next, layer your clothes on the hangers in the following methods:

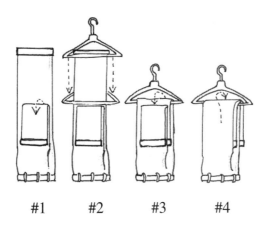

#1   #2   #3   #4

#1 Place pants on a flat surface and fold top pant leg back in half
#2 Slip hanger on bottom pant leg to knee
#3 Fold bottom pant leg to crotch over the hanger
#4 Fold top pant leg over the hanger and the other pant leg

This method secures the pants to the hanger without needing clothes pins or safety pins.

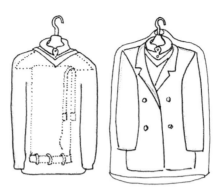

Next place shirts (buttoning articles as you go along) over the pants (and jackets if applicable). Cover each hanger with dry-cleaner bags once all the clothes have been hung on it.

Place dresses on the next hanger and cover them with dry-cleaner bags helping to protect them and keep wrinkles to a minimum.

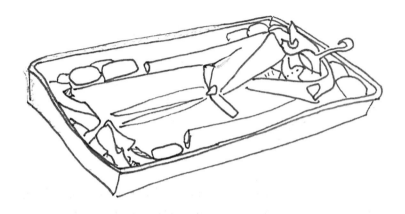

After you have all your clothes on the hangers, place your robe or overcoat around all of the clothing. Place this bundle inside your garment bag.

Gently fold any garments up at the bottom if they are longer than the garment bag. (Secure the strap of the garment bag around the center of the "bundle" if provided).

In the additional packing area around the hangers, stuff the corners with either socks and shoes or knit clothes that have been rolled up. Be sure to pad high-heeled shoes or any sharp items so as not to poke through the bag.

The biggest mistake most people make when they pack garment bags is that they don't pack enough to keep items from shifting and everything falls to the bottom of the bag.

Additional Hints for Packing A Garment Bag:

- Twist-tie hangers together if they are not those that originally came with the bag. This will keep them from falling and snagging clothes on the way down.

- Place those garments that wrinkle easily, at the back of the bag (closest to the outside). In this way, they will have less pressure and be less likely to wrinkle. Don't overpack your garment bag or it will be very cumbersome to carry.

- Don't forget luggage straps that are used mainly around the girth of hardsided luggage. These are terrific to keep your garment bag together, especially when you're carrying it. Be sure to secure the hook inside your bag by either snapping it in the original closing or by using a piece of string or a twist-tie. (A porter once said that the best way to guarantee you'll never see your bag again is to have it hook one of them as they transfer it).

- Purchase inexpensive locks to help keep zippers closed on outside pockets of your garment bag.

- When checking a garment bag at the airport, be sure to ask at the ticket counter for a cardboard box to help protect it. Some airlines provide these free of charge; they help keep your bag looking new.

- When carrying your garment bag on the plane, make sure that it is hung near your seat. Often, the closets are filled and the flight attendants must take your bag to the opposite end of the plane. If this happens, request that your bag be brought to your area before the plane starts deplaning procedures, so you may deplane as soon as possible.

- Also, don't pack valuables in your garment bag in case it is moved out of sight, either on the plane or on land.

General Packing Tips

- First, make a list of all the items that you want to take with you as you think of them. Check off these items as you pack. Keep this packing list and use it as a reference for your next trip.

- Another idea is to list all the activities that you will be attending while you are away. Now, list what clothes and accessories you need. Start by laying out your items on an extra bed or couch as you think of them.

- Place all your clothes for the trip out then place *half* of them back in the closet.

- Take *half* the amount of clothes and *twice* the money!

- Only pack what you can carry around your block without putting down, or for one mile. This gives you a good idea of what you will encounter in an airport without porters.

- Inter-pack your luggage with your traveling companion: Just in case one piece is missing or delayed, you will still have a few items of your own. This idea also applies to traveling alone and "scattering" your casual, semi-formal, and formal clothes between your various cases. Some may find this impractical, but it works!

- Always pack lots of plastic bags in varying sizes to hold jewelry, wet swimsuits, cosmetics, and laundry.

- Pack your toiletries one to two days in advance and then go through your normal routine. Check to make sure that everything you need is ready to go. Remember that trial sizes of almost everything save space. Who needs 12 ounces of shampoo for a one-week trip?

- Do not fill bottles to the top with liquids. Squeeze out excess air and put tape around the top for added protection.

- For security sake, do not carry anything for anyone for any reason.

- If you're pressed for space, wear your heaviest clothing instead of packing it.

- Pack your underclothes in mesh laundry bags to save space and make clothes easily available for washing.

- Don't forget the old trick of hanging wrinkled items in a bathroom full of steam to help freshen them up.

- Save the inserts of perfume and cologne samples from magazines and your monthly bills to use when traveling. You won't have to worry about bottles breaking.

·5·

Travel Documents and Money Safety

The most important suggestion regarding money and documents for a trip is: start to plan early. Too often we hear nightmare accounts of friends forgetting to apply for a passport or visa well in advance and they wind up anxiously awaiting the arrival of the document, hoping their trip will not be in jeopardy.

Once you have your passport, visas, and inoculations, the following suggestions will help you avoid misfortunes along your way:

- Be sure to always carry your passport with you for ease in cashing travelers checks.

- Super glue a small piece of Ultra Suede to the back side of your passport so it won't slip out of your purse or passport carrier easily. Velcro will also work.

- Before buying travelers checks, check into places that may give them to you free: American Express, AAA, or your own bank.

- Take travelers checks in both the husband and wife's name for ease in cashing.

- Share travelers checks between husband and wife or traveling companions in case of unwanted separation or theft.

- If traveling to many countries, consider purchasing your travelers checks in smaller denominations, making it easier to use up all the currency before you leave. And when moving from country to country quickly, you don't need to spend as much time converting left-over change.

- Alternatively, if you will be visiting only a few countries and spending a great deal of money on large purchases, then it would be more sensible and beneficial to obtain travelers checks in large denominations, or consider using a credit card, which may insure the purchase as well.

- Travel only with the major credit cards you plan on using or will need in case of an emergency. Leave all others at home.

- Consider purchasing your airline ticket with a major credit card in case the airline goes under and you lose your money. A credit card company usually has larger resources for such situations so you're not out the money in the meantime.

- When traveling with a companion, make sure that each of you takes different credit cards, if they are in the same name. Therefore, if one is stolen and you must cancel it for fear of someone using it, you will have a back-up card. Also, you will have a higher total credit limit on two cards than on one, just in case you decide to extend your holiday.

- If you are a serious shopper and think that you'll spend everything at the onset of your holiday, consider sending money to designated destinations on your itinerary.

- Take a small amount of currency ($50-$100) in the country's local currency for arrival, in case the banks are closed and you need it for porters, taxies, or buses.

- Call your bank prior to leaving and receive the current exchange rates of the countries you're traveling to. Write them down and keep them in your wallet for quick reference.

- Don't forget to take a small amount of your own country's currency to use upon departure and arrival from your home city.

- Carry small amounts (50 cents to $1.00) in the currency of the country you are going to for bathroom attendants. This is a custom of many countries and is a must to receive toilet paper.

- Keep a few $1.00 bills in your pocket for tipping so you don't need to open your purse or wallet.

- Tear up your carbon copies from your credit card purchases. This helps assure that no one can find your credit card number and misuse it.

·6·

Cruising Tips

Cruising is now one of the most popular holiday choices offered to travelers. Although cruises have been around for years, there are now many more lines and itineraries to choose from. These days, it seems like everyone is cruising.

The majority of cruise lines do not have specific luggage allowances, but it is recommended to check with your travel agent and/or airline to see what your air allowances are.

The benefit of a cruise holiday is that almost every detail of your trip is taken care of for you. As most cruises are sold exclusively through travel agents, once you have decided which one is for you, you can relax and leave the planning to them.

It is a good idea to be familiar with your cruise line's brochure and know exactly what is and what is not included in the price. This varies greatly from line to line. For example, some cruise lines include your shore excursions in the total cruise fare, while most do not, and this can make a huge difference in price if you intend to take advantage of the ship's tour program.

Following are some helpful hints to assist you in deciding which cruise program is right for you:

Organizing Your Cruise Wardrobe

- Remember that black is always formal. You can dress-up an outfit many different ways with just a minimal amount of accessories when you wear black, and save purchasing additional clothes.

- Many people choose cruising as a holiday because they enjoy "dressing" for dinner and having the opportunity to wear fine jewelry. This seems to work well for most people, but remember that you must get to the ship via airplanes, buses, etc., and it should be kept in the ship's safety vault when you're not wearing it. This is very time consuming and worrisome, so it is suggested that you carefully weigh the pros and cons of bringing valuables on your cruise.

- Ask your travel agent to find out specifically how many casual, semi-formal, and formal nights your cruise will have. This varies from line to line and itinerary. Make a list of each and what clothes you plan to wear . This cuts down on over-packing.

- Make a list of all the Theme Nights that you would like to participate in, and list the clothing you might take for them. For example, cruise lines often have a 50's & 60's night, Country/Western night, or an Island Deck Party. Ask your friends and relatives if they have an item of clothing that you can borrow before you purchase something that you probably won't wear again in the near future.

- The potential expense of a cruise wardrobe is the formal attire. Women passengers wear almost anything from nice dresses to exquisite sequin gowns. Unless a gentleman is very comfortable in and enjoys wearing a tuxedo, it is not necessary to bring one. A dark suit with a nice tie works fine. Usually the longer the cruise the fancier the dress is, but even that rule of thumb is variable.

- For formal night, a woman would feel quite acceptable in a medium-to-long dress, or a skirt with a fancy top/ blouse. A black skirt works well, as you can change many different tops and belts to dress it up or down. As well, a pair of fancy black pants with silk/polyester blouses and low black heels can turn simpler clothes into a variety of looks.

- Don't forget opera-length pearls, which can add that extra touch of glamour. They can be shortened with a pearl clip to change the effect. Matching earrings with a bit of rhinestone look very elegant.

- Rhinestone necklaces and bracelets are fun to wear and can be expensive to buy. Ask someone who just returned from a cruise if they might have some you could borrow, or check second-hand stores for a great savings.

- Don't forget an evening clutch bag or one with a strap. Again, stay with a basic color scheme and check your department or vintage clothing store for specials. These are usually sold in the boutiques on board in case you forget yours or would rather wait to see their selection.

- If you are on a clothing budget, ask friends and family to lend you some fancy things they may have just sitting around the house. And check into formal wear rentals for women as well as men.

Generally, there are three "categories" of evening dress on board:

Casual
Casual means exactly what it says, comfortable clothing. But not sweatsuits. Some cruise lines allow dressy jeans in the dining room for dinner, but not all. Check with your travel agent.

Semi Formal or Informal
For ladies, dresses or blouses and slacks are suggested. For men, usually jackets are required, ties optional.

Formal
Cocktail dresses or gowns for ladies, and tuxedos or business suits suggested for men (usually jackets and ties required).

- Ask your travel agent for suggestions if you need additional advice or ask him/her to refer you to a client that has just returned from the cruise line you are sailing on. First hand knowledge is invaluable.

- Most importantly, take into consideration the type of cruising that you will be doing. Obviously, a weekend cruise is more casual overall than a world cruise.

General Cruising Tips

- When you pack your carry-on for a cruise holiday, try packing everything you will need for the first three days in this bag. With the chance of lost or delayed luggage, especially if you arrive at your destination the same day you set sail, you may sail without your checked luggage. This is, of course, a suggestion only for those people who would be overwhelmed at the prospect of their luggage being delayed. If not, then pack as you feel comfortable.

- Highly suggested is arriving at least one day in advance to give your luggage the chance to catch up with you and to allow you to begin your holiday a bit more rested and relaxed. This would most probably be at an additional expense to you, but ask your travel agent if it's a possibility. This also gives you time to tour the port of sailing, as usually you sail immediately. Check into the pre- and post- cruise packages that most cruise lines offer, usually at a terrific savings.

- Pack an outfit that can double as exercise wear. Many passengers discover great programs onboard designed for all levels of fitness for example, a walk-a-mile class and wish they had brought something to exercise in. It's a great way to meet friends and also justify that second helping of cherries jubilee the night before!

- If you are a serious exercise enthusiast, check into different cruise lines. Most offer fantastic exercise programs and state of-the-art gym equipment. On some lines, entire theme cruises are planned around the exercise program. Be sure to confirm that the ship you choose has a fitness director onboard. Some ships even have incentive programs in which you are awarded gifts for your participation.

- Ships' activities are a great way to meet new friends. All lines' activities vary, so ask your travel agent if he/ she has a recent copy of the daily activities program from the ship you are looking into. Arts and crafts classes, solo-travelers get togethers, almost everything is offered. Once aboard, ask the cruise staff if they have such activities planned.

- Bring a bathing cap to double as a shower cap if needed. Many cruise ship swimming pools are salt water, which can be damaging to your hair if it's chemically treated or very dry. Take extra hair conditioner along just in case.

- A shawl or large scarf is a must if you tend to chill easily. Whether for a nice stroll out on deck under the stars or for the air-conditioning in the lounges, you'll be glad that you brought it. Black is a good color choice as it can be used on formal nights as well. (White can function this way too, but shows dirt more easily.)

- Of course, you should always pack comfortable shoes when traveling but do so especially on a ship that is constantly moving. High heels can be very dangerous. A dressy low heel is much more practical.

- Expandable wasted clothes are essential for those who enjoy eating (and that's one of the main attractions of a cruise)!

- A sarong makes a handy cover-up for the pool or beach. It's easy to tie on and wear while sitting at the counter for a refreshing drink, or to throw over you when you've had enough sun.

- If you are traveling with children or grandchildren, make sure that the ship you are on encourages them. There are certain lines that specialize in children's programs with entire daily schedules printed just for them. Generally, the peak cruising times for children are the holidays: Christmas/Hanukkah , Easter/ Spring Break, Summer, and Thanksgiving. If you prefer the company of adults only, heed this last information and choose your schedule accordingly.

- As the sun's rays are much stronger at sea than on land due to the lack of pollution and clouds screening out the sun's harmful rays, wear extra suntan lotion and a head covering if you are susceptible to burns. A visor is helpful if you like to read in the sun, and don't forget the effects of sun reflected off water if you are poolside or at the beach. The same effect exists with snow on the colder itineraries such as Alaska and Scandinavia.

- Throw in the novel that you haven't had time to read yet. Most ships have excellent libraries, but on the chance that yours doesn't, take it along. A tip on ships' libraries: check out the book selection as soon as you have a chance. Passengers tend to linger over books that they've borrowed, and the selection is greatly reduced after the first few days at sea.

- Instead of packing your old paperback to take home, suggest a paperback exchange, if there isn't one already set-up by the staff. A great way to meet someone and trade your old book for a new one for the trip home.

- If you do forget something, remember that the ship's boutique usually has any item that you may need. In addition, check their daily specials. Even on cruises with ideal shopping destinations, remember that the ship's boutiques have competitive prices.

- If you wear pantyhose, bring a few pairs with you. This is one article of clothing that varies greatly from one brand to another, especially the size.

- If you must iron your clothes, ask your travel agent about the availability of ironing rooms on your chosen ship. Most cruise lines discourage bringing your own iron due to the safety factor involved. Also, if the ship is an older one, make sure that you will have outlets that accommodate the voltage of your various appliances in your cabin.

- Each day you will receive a log of the daily activities that will take place with the time and location listed. It is a good idea to read this every evening so you don't miss out on any activities that may interest you. If you're not sure of your way around the ship, and did not receive a map upon embarkation, ask the front office for one to assist you in getting around.

- The radio room usually prints a capsule of the day's news happening around the world. Also, check the ships library to see if any newspapers were brought aboard in port.

- If for some reason you are disappointed with some aspect of your cruise, inform the front office immediately. The majority of the time it can be solved with ease.

- The majority of all cruise lines have a "Sign-As-You-Sail" policy for all purchases made onboard. You simply sign your name and cabin or account number, and show your ship's account card, which doubles as a boarding pass in most instances. You may choose to add a gratuity on the bottom of the check, if it has not been added automatically.

- For ease in settling your account, most cruise lines encourage you to leave an imprint of your major credit card with the front office during the first few days of the cruise. Your itemized bill will be sent to your cabin directly, usually the day before you disembark for approval and inspection. This eliminates standing in line on the last day.

Seasickness

With today's modern technology and stabilizers, there is little chance of seasickness. But, if you are susceptible to motion sickness, be sure to check with your physician before leaving home. There are many different products on the market to help, including pills and patches, though these may have different side effects for different people.

Sea Bands, a non-medicinal aid for seasickness, is a favorite among many passengers. They are elasticized wrist bands that apply slight pressure on the accupressure point near each wrist that helps controls nausea.

A few suggestions to help queasy stomachs: Dry foods, such as bread, breadsticks, or crackers, help to settle the uneasy feeling experienced in rough seas. Also limiting intake of liquids is suggested.

Safety At Sea

- A General Muster Drill is held the first day on most cruise ships, in compliance with United States Coast Guard requirements and local authorities. This is for the safety of all passengers and crew, and everyone is required to attend. Prior to the drill, there is a general announcement or written explanation of what you are specifically required to do.

- Once you are in your cabin, check to see where the nearest fire doors and stairs are and also locate your lifejacket. Familiarize yourself with wearing your lifejacket correctly.

- If you are unable to climb stairs, let the front office and your cabin steward know that you may need extra assistance in an emergency. As the Boy Scouts say, "Be Prepared."

- Large cruise ships are all equipped with a hospital and medical staff. There is a nominal charge for being seen and prescriptions.

Selecting a Cabin

- Your travel agent is the most important wealth of knowledge for all your travel needs. But you must provide some information about yourself so he/she can find the cabin best suited to your needs. Here are some suggestions:

- If you tend to get seasick or think you might, a mid-ships cabin would be a good idea. Away from the pitching and rolling of the topside and lower decks, you will be the most stable.

- If you use a wheelchair, make sure that your cabin and bathroom are accessible. And make sure there is an elevator in the vicinity. Read the diagram in the brochure to find out about the layout of the ship and ask your travel agent's advice, too.

- Do you want/need a TV, a suite or verandah? Check the prices in the different categories. A porthole? If you don't plan on spending much time in your cabin, a porthole is an added expense that you may not need.

- Are you a light sleeper? Check where the lounges are located, as a late-night band might keep you awake.

- If you prefer a queen or king size bed, make sure that the ship you have chosen can accommodate your request. Some of the older ships are furnished with only twin beds.

Dining Tips

- Most cruise ships offer you the choice of two sittings generally called *early* and *late*. The early sitting usually begins at 6 p.m. and the late around 8 p.m. As usually your evenings' entertainment follows your dinner, second sitting is generally for the younger or more late-night sort of person who enjoys a show beginning usually after 10 p.m. The first sitting show usually begins around 8 p.m.

- If you do have a preference in sittings, be sure to request it from your travel agent. Remember, though, that requests cannot always be accommodated, though the line will try to do so if at all possible.

- Also, request to sit with any specific friends you are traveling with. Table size runs anywhere from an intimate table for two to a large table of eight. Many passengers prefer a large table, using the philosophy that out of eight people chances are there will be some that are interesting conversationalists .

- If you have received your seating arrangements and they are not what you requested, contact the Maitre d' as soon as possible (or the person in charge of the sitting assignments). For some passengers, this is the most important part of their cruise. Remember, a smile and a polite handshake go a long distance to remedy a situation.

- If you have special dietary requirements, request these when you are booking your cruise. Make sure that the ship you want can accommodate your requirements. As with most airlines, generally all cruise ships are capable of providing low sodium and vegetarian meals. Remember that this is an extra service, so patience and understanding go a long way during the first few meals with a new waiter.

Tips on Tipping

- Tipping varies greatly from ship to ship for which service was performed and how. Some cruise lines have a "No tipping required" policy, however, most passengers choose to extend gratuities for a job well done. Generally, you will receive with your documents an updated guideline regarding who, when, and how much you should tip, so you know ahead of time how much money to take with you, and if in doubt, ask once you are onboard. Following is a very general outline based on per person per day of your cruise:

- Cabin steward $3 per person per day
- Asst. steward $1.75 per person per day
- Dining room waiter $3 per person per day
- Bus boy $1.75 per person per day

- Also, tipping of the maitre d' and the head waiter for any special meals or assistance is customary. Tipping for wine stewards is recommended at 15-20 percent. A note: If you receive a complimentary bottle of wine, it is customary to tip the wine steward for this service as if you had purchased the wine yourself.

- When ordering drinks on deck or in the dining room, check to see if a gratuity has automatically been added or ask the bartender. Sometimes it is added for your convenience. If not, and you wish to add a gratuity, you may do so each time you are served. Some passengers prefer to wait until the end of the cruise to personally tip a favorite bartender/waiter.

- When to tip? The majority of passengers wait until the last evening of the cruise and personally thank the person for making their cruise so memorable. Envelopes are provided at the front office for your convenience.

- Towards the end of the cruise, you will receive a comment form on which you may express your compliments and comments regarding your cruise. These are taken very seriously as an over-view of how the ship is meeting your standards, and your opinions are directly reflected to the shoreside management. It is appreciated when passengers take the time to fill them out and pass on compliments where they see fit.

- At the end of the cruise, usually the second to the last day, a disembarkation talk for all passengers is held. It is highly suggested that one member of each party or family attends. Information is given regarding disembarkation procedures, customs, luggage tags, airline connections and so on.

·7·

Travel Scarf Tying

A scarf is the most versatile accessory in your travel wardrobe. It can redefine any look and create styles that are casual or formal, professional or sporty.

By including the following scarves in your travels and using this chapter as your guide, you will learn how to extend your wardrobe without using valuable luggage space. You will also add glamour to your wardrobe without spending a lot of money.

These are three scarves that you should not leave home without. The style, size and method of tying is the real secret.

- **Oblong**   **10" x 54"**
- **Square**   **34" x 34**
- **Pareo**   **46" x 60"**

Scarf Tips:
- Pack scarves in plactic bags to keep wrinkles to a minimum.
- Silk scarves and natural fabrics are warmer than synthetics. Tuck them around the neck of a sweater to keep warm.
- Scarves make great gifts. They pack flat and don't break.
- The quality of scarves vary greatly. Look for scarf edges that are rolled and stitched by hand, usually indicating a higher quality of scarf than those stitched by machine.

Orient Express

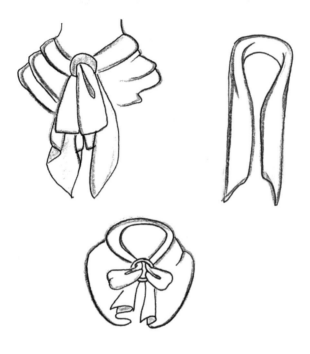

1. Drape oblong scarf around your neck 2. Pinch the inside edges of scarf at mid-way 3. Using a scarf clip or small rubber band, pull the edges slowly through until it forms a bow

As the name implies, this is a fast and elegant enhancement to any outfit. Works well with either silk or synthetic fabric. Small rubber-band weighs less than a scarf-clip and usually works better.

Parisienne Glamour

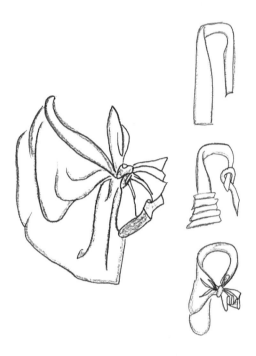

1. Place oblong scarf around neck keeping one end shorter than the other
2. Tie a loose knot in the short end
3. Fan pleat the long end up until it's even with the short end
4. Hold pleats together on the inside and push up half-way through the knot
5. Tighten the knot and fan as desired

This works well with light metallic fabrics. Worn with basic black or navy it is perfect for formal occasions.

Segovian Secret

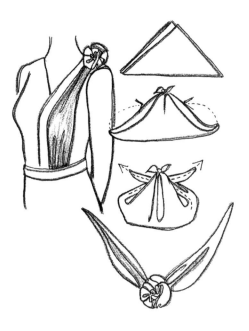

1. Fold square scarf into triangle and tie a small knot in top corner
2. Take opposite ends and cross beneath the small knot, exchange hands
3. Holding the ends, gently let the weight of the knot slowly slide down until the "rose " is formed
4. Drape over shoulder for a dramatic effect or around neck, waist or brim of hat

Works best with a silk scarf. Try a few different scarves to see varying results. Use a small safety pin to secure "rose" to garment.

English Accent

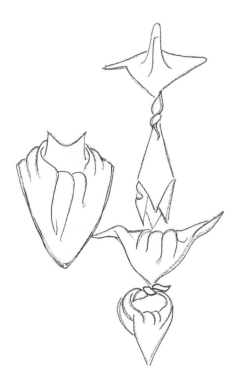

1. Place square scarf on a flat surface, wrong side up
2. Tie a small knot at the center & fold scarf into a triangle with the knot on the inside
3. Place the triangle in the front of the neck and tie at the back of the neck
4. Arrange drape as desired

Can be used as a substitute blouse under a V-neck sweater, cardigan or blazer. Perfect when traveling and laundry facilities are no where in sight!

St. Tropez Nights

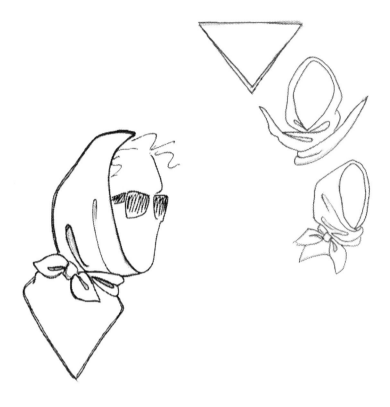

1. Fold a square scarf into a triangle
2. Drape over head and cross the ends under chin
3. Bring ends around to the back of neck and tie

A touch of glamour, works well with any type of fabric. Good for a walk around deck, with or without inclement weather!

Patagonia Cover

1. Place square scarf right side up on a flat surface
2. Fold the bottom edge to the top and then back in half
3. Taking bottom corners, turn scarf over, away from you
4. Place finger at the top corner and fold top two corners down to the bottom edge
5. From bottom, tightly roll all edges up until opening appears underneath
6. Drape on head and tie under chin. Fold back edge framing face.

Works well with any type of fabric. For warmth in very cold weather, use wool scarf instead of packing a wool hat. Saves space and your hairstyle.

North Cape

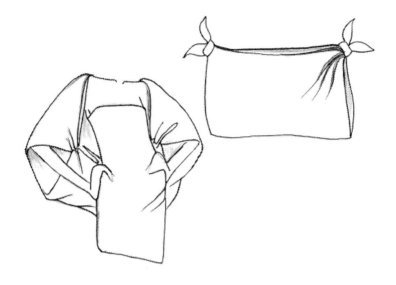

1. Fold pareo right sides together into a rectangle
2. Tie the two corners together on each end
3. Turn the pareo right side out and place your arms through the openings, keeping the knots under your arms

This is great for taking cover from the hot tropic sun, or keeping warm in air-conditioned restaurants. For a more formal look, use a fancier pareo or make one by simply cutting any type of fabric and finishing the edges. (An interesting outing in a foreign country is to a fabric store. Thai silk works beautifully).

Tahitian Pareo

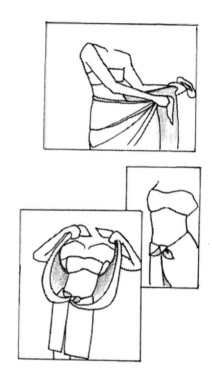

1. Fold pareo in half right sides together
2. Place fold at waist and knot
3. Take top layer from bottom edge and knot under your arm

Always travel with a cotton pareo to use as a cover-up, beach towel or as a light blanket in a pinch.

· 8 ·

Plane and Train Travel

Traveling is so easy these days and there are so many
different forms of transportation. Your best bet is to arrive
at your destination rested and relaxed, so you can start your
holiday immediately, or with a small amount of rest time.
Following are suggestions on how you can effectively and
comfortably travel while saving energy en route.

Planes

- Pack a pair of "sockettes" in your carry-on to put on
  after you take off your shoes. Saves your feet from
  swelling and keeps your toes warm.

- To help avoid jet lag, restrict your intake of alcohol and
  caffeine. Eat bland foods a few days before the trip, and
  do not eat spicy foods en route.

- Another helpful hint to stop jet lag: Adjust your
  sleeping habits before leaving home. Check the time
  zone to which you're headed and go to sleep an hour
  earlier than usual (or later, depending on which
  direction). Allow your body to adjust.

- When flying, avoid vast amounts of salt, which causes
  swelling in extremities, especially ankles.

- For contact wearers: Carry a travel-sized bottle of your
  saline solution in your carry-on. The air on planes tends
  to dry out the contact lens at high elevations and also air
  conditioning affects them as well. Unless you smoke,
  sit as far away from the smoking section as possible.

- If you have a cold or any other physical problem that you are concerned about, be sure to consult your physician before any flight.

- At the ticket counter, always have the ticket agent confirm your return coupons, as well as reserve your seat if you don't already have one.

- Check your baggage claim tickets immediately when they are stapled into your ticket jacket and attached to your luggage. Make sure that they match and that you have all of them. Everyone makes mistakes, and it's easier to catch them right away.

- Before leaving home for the airport, always call to find out if your flight is on time. Do so likewise when picking someone up at the airport, for often weather conditions cause delays, and you shouldn't spend needless time (and money for parking) waiting for their arrival.

- Once you are at the airport, check the monitors to see if your flight is still on time.

- Spend your time in the airport wisely. Use it to check out the different shops, which now include bookstores, card stores, and various specialty boutiques.

- In large airports where you may have to change terminals to catch your next flight, inquire about a shuttle service before deplaning. This saves times and allows you to head directly to the shuttle once you've landed.

- Many people prefer to wear casual clothing and then change in the airport restroom before claiming their baggage (especially on long international flights). The key here is to be comfortable.

- A window seat is best for sleeping. No one will crawl over you to get to the restroom or the overhead compartment.

- An aisle seat is best for stretching your legs and for those who may need to use the facilities often.

- Request a bulkhead seat or a row that is situated in front of an emergency exit for more leg room. (A bulkhead seat is a good idea if you are traveling with children, or a wheelchair or cane.) Also keep in mind that you may be sitting beside people with special needs and may be interrupted often.

- Bring your own pillowcase and place the pillow provided by the plane in it. This assures you of a comfortable rest and a feeling of home along the trip.

- Ask immediately upon embarking the plane for: a pillow, a blanket, and any magazines or newspapers. These items tend to run low during a full flight, and you have the largest selection if you inquire early.

- Ask the flight staff if the plane is fully booked. If not, you may be able to make yourself more comfortable by moving to another area of the plane to stretch out.

- The best solution many have found to keep ears clear while flying is to chew gum. Use it on both the ascent and descent.

- Pack eye-covers and ear-plugs for uninterrupted sleep while flying.

- An inflatable neck pillow (like the ones for cars) is perfect to save your neck from kinks.

- An airplane pillow used at the small of the back greatly relieves tired shoulders.

- To avoid a chance selection of only meat, request a fruit or green salad. Also available on most airlines are: low sodium meals, Kosher meals, low calorie meals, and more. Call your travel agent or airline directly to request one. Be sure to confirm at the check-in counter that your request was received.

- Take your seat immediately when they begin to start boarding your row on the plane. This way you are almost guaranteed your seat in case of over-booking, as you will already be sitting in it!

- Always leave your shoes on until the aircraft has reached cruising altitude- just in case you have to evacuate the aircraft in an emergency.

- Bring a large safety pin to "pin" your jacket to the seat in front of you. No need to bother hanging it up to be retrieved upon arrival.

- Keep a small spray bottle of water in your carry-on to keep your face and arms moisturized at high elevations. Also a travel-sized bottle of lotion and eye drops are great.

- To keep the circulation going in your legs, put your feet on your carry-on bag. (Of course make sure that you don't have any breakables near the surface).

- Be sure to drink plenty of water and juice; this keeps your body hydrated, especially in air conditioned enclosures.

- If your luggage is damaged, it should be reported as soon as possible to an airline representative before you leave the airport.

Train Travel

- In Europe, there is generally no luggage allowance on trains, though you must either check it in at the counter or carry it on with you. In either case, the same rule holds true: Less is better and easier. *Schlepping* suitcases and bags on and off trains with small aisles is not an enjoyable pastime.

- In America, Amtrak allows three checked bags per adult ticket. The maximum weight allowance may not exceed a total of 150 pounds. (Each bag should not weigh more than 74 pounds each). Check with the route and train that you'll be traveling on, as not all have baggage cars available.

- Generally, food is sold on trains. Of course, it is much more expensive than if purchased in a store, but the convenience is sometimes worth the price. If possible, it's fun to shop for a picnic lunch before arriving at the station and purchase hot beverages once onboard the train.

·9·
Security

The most important safety tip is to be aware of your surroundings. In this day and age, any city can be a place for thieves and burglars, even your own home town, no matter what size or population. The idea is not to travel in fear but to pay attention to some important details with which you can protect yourself, and your property, while you are traveling, and your home while you are away. Many of these following suggestions apply to everyday circumstances.

General Home Security

- Have your mail held at the post office for your return.

- Have your newspaper stopped. (Although people say that stopping the paper delivery can be a tip off to burglars.)

- Hire a gardener to take care of your garden and keep your lawn mowed.

- In cold climate zones, turn off your hot water heater and defrost the refrigerator in case of power failure. If you live in temperate climates, turn down your furnace and air conditioning.

- Leave timers on the lights in your house, and for a good deterrent, leave your radio tuned to a talk show.

- Unplug your appliances such as your computer, stereo, and television in case of power surges.

- Don't forget to also stop UPS delivery or any other service that usually frequents your home.

- Affix screws into window frames to secure them from outside opening. Ask at your hardware store for additional ideas.

- For added security to sliding glass doors, place a broom handle in the track. Also, a board across the center of the window placed on two rivets will do the same trick.

- If you have an answering machine, ask a friend to check it and answer any messages that sound important. Calls unreturned for any length of time are a good give-away that you are not at home.

- If you don't have an answering machine, put your telephone on the lowest ring setting so that no one outside can hear the continual ringing.

- Lock all your valuables in a safe deposit box.

- An engraving pen from your local library or police station is recommended for marking your valuable electronic equipment with an ID number.

The following are things you should ask a neighbor or relative to do while you are away to help give the appearance that you are home:

- Place their garbage in yours once in awhile.

- Shovel snow from your sidewalk and driveway.

- Park their car in your driveway after 5 pm in the evening and on the weekends once in awhile.

- Check your mailbox periodically for any mail or advertising that might have slipped through.

- Keep a set of your car keys in case there is a fire in your garage, or any other reason your cars need to be moved.

- Check the inside of your home periodically in case there has been any kind of water damage, frozen pipes, or anything that they might be able to assist with until you return home.

Security En Route

- Always use valet parking when available. Walking through a deserted parking lot alone is not a good idea anywhere. Be sure to give your car only to a uniformed valet.

- When checking into a hotel, be sure to only give your work address. Otherwise it is a sign to burglars that you are not at home.

- If the desk clerk announces loudly your room number, ask for a different one. Strangers may be within hearing and harass you later. Fortunately, hotels are aware of this and henceforth are very cautious.

- When traveling alone, always guarantee your hotel room reservation to a major credit card, just in case you are delayed on your flight or arriving transportation.

- When you are traveling alone, be sure to always have reservations.

- If available, request a room near the elevator, to avoid the chance of someone following you and walking long distances in empty hallways.

- Always leave the light on in your hotel room and the "Do Not Disturb" sign on the door (after the maid has cleaned) when you leave, to eliminate any unwanted visitors. And leave your TV turned on. While you are inside your hotel room, always keep the door locked (if it isn't automatically) and the chain across the lock (if provided).

- When dining alone, take a book or magazine to the table. This will make you feel more at ease eating alone.

- Ask what credit cards are accepted before dining or purchasing something. This saves embarrassing situations.

- There are a few different travel door alarms that pack easily and hang on your hotel door. When someone tries to open the door an alarm sounds. Many travelers use this as an inexpensive alarm on their front door while they are away *and* while they are home!

- Another alternative is an inexpensive door wedge for added protection in unfamiliar surroundings.

- In a hotel room or aboard ship, memorize the location of the nearest emergency exit. Count the number of doors in case of heavy smoke. You should also count the number of rows to the nearest exit on the plane in case the lights go out.

- If you have an uneasy feeling about a hotel, don't hang the "Make Up My Room" on your door. Instead, locate the maid and advise that you'd like your room cleaned and that the "Do Not Disturb" sign be hung on the door when finished. Any steps that you can take to help secure yourself and your surroundings are worth the extra bit of time and effort.

- Don't leave any valuables in your room when you leave. Experienced thieves know how to find what they're looking for. Place them in the management's safe keeping place.

- Use the "peep-hole" in your door to see who is there before opening it. If you are the least bit uncomfortable, call the front desk immediately.

- Most hotels no longer print the room numbers of the keys, but in the event that they do, be sure not to leave your key in any position where strangers could see your room number. This could lead to problems later on.

- If you are a single woman traveler and find yourself in the situation of a foreign man harassing you, sit beside a native woman on the train or bus, or walk directly behind women. Even though there often is a language barrier, women tend to stick together and can understand a look of distress towards an overly friendly male pursuer.

- When traveling alone, sit in the front of the transportation to be able to ask directions.

· 10 ·

General Travel Tips

Over the years, I have picked up numerous travel and packing tips from the travelers that I have met along my journeys. From solo travelers to cruise passengers to tour members, they passed on the following hints and swear to their effectiveness in making their trip just a little bit easier. Hopefully even the seasoned traveler can pick up a few new travel tips.

- Be sure to break in any new shoes before leaving home.

- Don't forget to take a small packet of cold water soap just in case you find hot water unavailable.

- Fake pearls make a very elegant statement and look just as nice as real ones without the worry.

- If you must take valuables with you, be sure to store them in the hotel or ship's safe, generally free of charge and much safer than your room.

- Remember to take items that can double for other uses: a raincoat can act as a blanket on a train or bus. A large T-shirt can be used for a nightgown, exercises, or cover-up as well.

- Don't overlook the need for some real casual clothes like your favorite sweats, T-Shirts, and tennis shoes. These are great for relaxing around the hotel room, exercising, or for long traveling days.

- Shop periodically for trial size items you know you will eventually need, and put them away for your upcoming trip. No need to spend time decanting large bottles to small ones.

- Obtain a calling card or code number from your long distance telephone company before leaving home. This will expedite any calls you must make and put an end to searching for correct coins in foreign currency.

- Take a nightlight for unfamiliar hotel rooms or cabins.

- Sample sizes of dishwashing liquid, mailed as promotions, are great for getting grease out of clothes, and they are packaged not to break.

- Hairspray makes for a quick room freshener in a pinch.

- On your travels, collect samples like shampoo and soap from hotel rooms and bring them home, even if not to your taste. (A frequent traveler says she places them all in small travel bags and gave one collection to a friend for a bon voyage gift.) Alternately, keep them for visiting guests to your home or donate to a local shelter.

- Keep a list of all the receipts from your purchases for your return home through customs. For ease, record them in your travel diary at the end of each day, and save time by writing once at the end of each day: about your travels and keeping track of expenditures at the same time.

- Pack all your purchases in the same piece of luggage in case customs asks to see them. This saves time and embarrassment digging for them!

- Use a picture of your family as a bookmark. This is a nice reminder of those at home and a good conversation starter!

- Save clean napkins from the breakfast table for your day's journey. They can provide a quick clean up!

- A card with typed telephone numbers and names of relatives, bank account, insurance company, etc., can be very helpful in case of an emergency.

- Be sure that your bills are paid and up to date if you plan to be gone for an extended period of time.

- Photocopy the pages in your travel guide for your own use so you don't have to take the entire book along. Or simply tear out the applicable chapters.

- Develop at least one roll of film at the beginning of your holiday to ensure that your camera is still functioning. This is important for both new and old cameras alike.

- Check batteries in your travel flashlight and remove them when not in use. For emergencies, place the flashlight near your bed when going to sleep.

- Don't forget to take extra batteries for *everything*. They may be impossible to find, and also expensive, in certain countries. You don't want to waste precious sightseeing time in a frustrating search. This includes hearing aid batteries.

- Place a small round identifying sticker on the upper right-hand corner of your passport (outside) so it's easier to distinguish when traveling with a group.

- Check the expiration dates on your credit cards, passport, driver's license, medical certificates, camera film, vitamins, medications, etc.

Recycling 35 MM Film Canisters

Fill your empty film canisters with laundry soap and use the cap to seal and prevent it from spilling. Toss when empty.

Use clear film canisters to keep change together when traveling to many different countries on a single trip.

Empty film canisters also make perfect containers for safety pins, sewing kits, and numerous other items.

Number your film containers as you take pictures and make a list of what each roll contains. Place your exposed film back in the original container. This will make recording your trip much easier once you're home.

- Check with your pet sitters, plant sitters, and child care. Have a second choice on standby just in case someone has to cancel at the last minute.

- Use blank index cards or recipe cards to record special events on them, such as birthdays and anniversaries that will occur while you're away.

- Bring along special event cards for birthdays, Christmas, Hanukkah, and so on. This saves last minute shopping time in strange cities, not to mention the possible unavailability of English cards. Unless, of course, you like the charm of cards in another language. They make a nice souvenir!

- Concierge at major hotels are an invaluable source of information.

- Put your name and business address in your overcoat. They are always being left in restaurants, planes, and trains.

- Purchase some sticky address labels and spend an evening addressing them to all your family and friends before your trip. When you are traveling, no need to haul your address book with you. Just peel and stick. Easier and faster.

- For those travelers who tend to get cold easily: Lightweight (nylon outside, cotton inside) long underwear, available in two piece sets (or silk more expensive) fits well under any type of clothing; they're easy to pack and launder and keep you warm.

- If you have allergic reactions to certain foods, have someone write on a card, in the language of the countries that you are visiting, the foods you cannot eat.

- If you have a serious medical problem, be sure to check with your physician about possible problems and facilities abroad.

- Keep a MedicAlert card in your wallet or purse if you have a medical problem or allergies. It is also advisable to put your blood type on it.

- Update any prescriptions and take extra with you. Be sure to keep all medicine in their original, labeled bottles to avoid problems.

- While some people consider it a challenge to bring undeclared items through customs, this can be a disastrous and expensive ending to a nice trip.

- A metal Band-Aid box makes a great first-aid box. Fill it with all the supplies you may need.

- Rubber-soled shoes should be taken for marble floors and cobblestone streets where it is easy to slip and fall.

- Secure the shoulder strap of your carry-on around your foot or chair leg when seated. This acts as an anchor if the bag is grabbed.

- Copy on recipe cards: jokes, riddles, songs, recipes, etc., to share with new friends and children along the way. If you have a special cake recipe and facilities are available, you can make one to share with foreigners.

- When looking for local activities in a foreign city, check out the daily newspaper. The TV guide section can be understood in almost any language.

- Small cosmetic bags with zippers make great places to keep costume jewelry, different currencies, and other small items.

- Cut a piece of plastic the same size as your face powder box and place it in the top. This prevents the powder from spilling.

- While traveling long distances, mail home paper "extras" and items accumulated along the way but don't want to throw out: city maps, tourist pamphlets, attraction stubs, and receipts for tax purposes. A good idea is to pack a manila envelope in your luggage and keep these items inside until you're ready to mail it home.

- When traveling alone, treat yourself to a nice bouquet of flowers to brighten up your hotel room.

- Request or reconfirm any additional assistance that you may need on your holiday: diet requirements, wheelchair assistance, special seating, etc.

- Take only jewelry that you can wear without worry. No need for a safety box and the effort of checking it in and out at the front desk.

- Always remember when packing your bags to pack your respect for people of different cultures. You will most often find that people throughout the world are happy to have you as a visitor -- as long as you are considerate of them and their way of life.

(The folk's at CARE, the non-profit relief organization, fully endorse this tip. For 50 years they have represented American generosity by helping people in need throughout the developing world. To find out more about CARE, please call 1-800-521-CARE.)

· 11 ·
Gift Ideas

Whether you are traveling to visit old friends, or just making new friends along the way, it is always a nice gesture to bring a gift. It need not be an expensive gift, and obviously, the easier it is to pack the better.

Keep in mind when you are selecting presents that anything with a place name or logo on it is treasured by foreigners. In addition, something with a picture of your home state or region is very interesting to others and leads to engaging conversation.

Before you leave home, make up a "gift list" of everyone you intend to remember with a gift. Start with the most important and continue down.

The following are a few tried and tested gift ideas.

Balloons An all-time favorite! Sailing into the San Blas Islands off Panama, a seasoned traveler always fills his/her short's pockets with balloons to give to the children. Unbreakable and fun to play with, hold them behind your back and have them guess what color the balloon is, and the first one who guesses correctly wins the balloon. If you do this, for example in Spanish, you then teach them the color in English. It can be done anywhere in the world in any language.

Crocheted Or Any Handmade Gift For those travelers who enjoy making things with their hands, take a crochet hook along and during long train rides and plane flights you can make small items like pot- holders. Then, as you travel and meet new friends, give them away. By purchasing your yarn along the way, you can try new patterns and keep yourself busy as well.

Frisbee A Frisbee, made out of a special material which packs flat, or else the standard plastic type, especially with printing on it from a sporting event or foreign country or large city, is a favorite gift. This also may begin a game or two along the route and is great exercise as well.

Inflatable Plastic Beach Ball Very easy to pack and a wonderful conversation starter with foreigners where there is a language barrier. It is also a godsend for crying children in small enclosed areas or waiting in line outdoors. A favorable theme for beach balls is cartoon characters. A very inexpensive, lightweight gift.

Picture Calendar A calendar from your home region is a greatly appreciated gift and a useful one. Packs flat on the bottom of your suitcase and allows you to show your hosts or new friends the beautiful areas near your home, which may be very different from their country.

Pins Any type, that are worn everywhere these days: hats, lapels, sweaters, anywhere. Small and easy to pack with anything from your local regatta to the state flower.

Pens In the Orient, pens are popular as a gift idea. A variety of colors and sizes is appreciated by all ages. They make good tips and gifts for people along the way, as many Asian customs do not allow monetary gratuities.

Polaroid Camera Take a Polaroid camera for instant pictures. Also a great icebreaker with new friends. A traveler in the Amazon took pictures of children along the route. He was glad that he had packed extra film: the entire tribe wanted their picture taken, and he was in no position to argue.

Scarf or Cap A pretty scarf, always light weight and easy to pack, is a nice gesture to a hostess. As well, a cap, with the logo of your favorite team or sport is great for a host.

Silk Corsage A silk corsage is an attractive and much appreciated gift. It won't wilt and packs easily. It is an especially good idea for a cruise or any holiday where there probably won't be a flower shop in the vicinity, saving a search for flowers at the last minute in an unfamiliar place

Silk Flowers The same idea as a corsage but to give as a gift to friends or family in whose home you are staying.

Stickers and Decals From elections, sporting events, or your own home town. Bumper stickers or decals that are often seen on trailers are fun for children as well as adults.

Wrapping Paper, Ribbon, and a Collapsible Box For special occasions or for mailing gifts home. This saves time looking in foreign cities and saves carrying home extra weight.

·12·
Unforgettables

Every traveler has their favorite items that they always pack for a trip. The items listed here are merely suggestions that may make your trip just a little bit easier and more comfortable.

Of course, only pack what you deem necessary, depending on your itinerary and specific needs and space. These items are listed alphabetically for ease in selecting.

Adapters can be confusing. If you must travel with electrical appliances, be sure to have the correct adapters and converters.

Atlas in small travel size. Assists you when you are trying to explain to someone where you live, etc.

Anti-Bacterial Wipes for quick clean-ups

Bag for miscellaneous Items such as: rubber bands, bobby pins, safety pins, Band-Aids, nail file, paper clips, extra buttons, extra small lock, extra luggage key.

Band-Aids in a few different sizes. These are better to have with you instead of searching for them and less expensive to purchase at home.

Bandanna in any color. A bandanna is very useful in many instances and emergencies: for repairing a bicycle, as a washcloth, as a head covering from cold or hot weather, to use as covering for a dirty bench before sitting, as a table cloth, anything!

Batteries for all of your equipment. They can be very expensive to purchase away from home and sometimes hard to find. Start to stock up for your holiday ahead of time and don't forget the batteries in your camera.

Belt Pack to secure all your daily items around your waist. This may be positioned in front to avoid anyone pick-pocketing you from the rear, or positioned in back for more comfort when you are away from civilization. Lightweight packs are available from most outdoor stores and catalogues.

Binoculars travel size that fit conveniently into a pocket. Great for spotting wildlife!

Book Light If you like to read after your room-mate goes to sleep or in a dark plane, train, etc. Also good for hotel rooms that may have poor lighting.

Book On Cassette and earphones to entertain you on long rides or flights when your eyes are tired and you can't sleep.

Boy Scout Kit complete with knife, spoon and fork, plate, and cup. Great for weekend trips in the car.

Bread Clips made of plastic that keep bread bags together. They work well for hanging laundry in hotel rooms and on the balcony railings, and they pack flat. Also can be used to hold draperies closed to keep light out (safety pins work here too).

Bubble Plastic that you receive in packages to avoid breakage. Take some along in a plastic bag to wrap any glass souvenirs you're bringing home.

Business Cards to exchange with new friends. It is never a good idea to give your home address to persons you have just met, nice as they may seem. It could fall into the hands of the wrong people.

Camera check the batteries and make sure that it's in good working condition.

Change Purse with several different compartments. *Baggallini* is a new brand which has five pockets, each with a different colored zipper. This is a great way to separate varying currencies without losing your patience.

Clothes Line to use for laundry as well as tying bags shut in an emergency. New ones are two pieces of elastic entwined, which eliminates the need for clothes pins.

Clothes Pins don't take up much room and you may need some.

Collapsible Cup for taking medicine, sharing a drink without the worry of germs.

Combination Locks are great for protecting your luggage from pilferage when it's out of sight.

Converter for electric shavers, curling irons, hot pot, etc. If possible, obtain appliances that run on batteries instead.

Denture Repair Kit containing instructions and materials for emergency repairs.

Dental Floss, which is very difficult to find in foreign countries. Also makes extremely strong thread for coats, jeans, and other tough items.

Dice to entertain you on long trips. Liar's Dice is a great game to play with train compartment companions and easy to learn.

Deodorant Stick-Ups for smelly hotel rooms, bathrooms, or even rental cars. (Of course, don't stick them to anything.) Quick, easy to use, and disposable.

Disposable Toiletries such as razors, cosmetics, toothpaste, soap, anything to lighten your load along the way.

Ear Plugs and Eye-Covers for traveling and ensuring sleep time. Great for noisy hotels, engine noise on planes.

Electric Razor that is battery operated. Can be used without electricity or water. Good for trains, planes, etc.

Eye Drops to soothe sore eyes on holiday. Keep in your carry-on for flying where air conditioning drys out eyes.

Eye Glass Repair Kit which is indispensable for those who wear glasses. Be sure it contains the proper screwdriver and screws.

Flashlight that is compact for use in emergencies. Good for hotel rooms, cabins, parking lots, and garages in case of blackouts. (Also excellent for reading menus in dark, romantic restaurants!) Get one with an ultra-shrill whistle incorporated for protection.

Flask preferably plastic for day trips, to fill with drinking water or whatever you choose. Inexpensive and lightweight.

Film for your camera or video camera. Check the expiration dates.

Folding Cane provides an extra bit of security for tired legs. Pack into a very compact size, perfect for traveling.

Guidebooks and Language Phrase Books

Hangers preferably plastic coated wire, for use in garment bags as well as closets. Plastic coated are better for washing and drying without rusting your clothes.

Hat of any comfortable material. Golf hats that roll up easily and pack to a minimum size are best. A must in hot climates.

Hot Pot might seem a bit extravagant, but for travelers who must have their coffee in the morning, this can be a godsend. Check the voltage requirements before purchasing. Saves the expense of ordering room service. Also when traveling with children, hot chocolate is a treat.

Hot Water Bottle for cold feet and sore muscles.

Inflatable Back Pillow designed specifically to support and position your lower back to avoid the ache that comes with sitting for long periods of time.

Inflatable Neck Pillow great neck support on long flights, trains and so on.

Inflatable Hangers fold into a tiny corner of your suitcase let your fine drip dry blouses, shirts, and sweaters dry quickly.

Iron or Steamer for wrinkles that you can't get out by hanging your clothes in a bathroom of hot steam. Only if you must take one with you. Check outlets and adapters before purchasing and packing.

Kaopectate and Lomotil (diarrhea medication) are priceless when traveling away from home. These brands have served many well, but if you have your own proven favorite, take it along to save problems on your trip.

Keys For Your Luggage carry extra keys to each suitcase. Carry one set of keys to your traveling companion's bags as well as your own, just in case your purse or carry-on is stolen or lost.

Key Chain with Flashlight makes it easy to see the lock in a dimly lit hallway or garage

Kleenex Packages in the small travel size. Can be used as toilet paper in emergencies and for quick clean ups.

Laundry Dryer Sheets keep your luggage smelling fresh and are super for removing static cling from your clothes. Just rub on pants, skirts, anything, and you're ready to go.

Luggage Straps great insurance against sprung hard sided luggage and great to help spotting your bag on the luggage carousel.

Magnifying Plastic to assist you in reading small-print maps, guidebooks, etc. Also handy for reading maps if you leave your glasses in your hotel room.

Marking Pen to identify your film canisters, for mailing parcels home, and to ID your articles along the way. Also, a highlighter is a good way to mark your guidebook or maps while traveling.

Medic Alert MedicAlert is an internationally recognized emergency medical identification system that communicates your special medical requirement needs. If you have a medical condition that others should be aware of in an emergency, you can contact the MedicAlert Foundation by dialing 1-800-ID-ALERT.

Medical Supplies and Medicine Always keep your pills in their original bottles with the prescription label on the outside. Do not use the Sunday, Monday, etc., pill boxes as customs personnel take a dim view of unlabeled pills.

Money Belt that secures snugly around your waist and made of lightweight nylon with zippered compartment for passport, large quantities of travelers checks, and major credit card. Sold at most luggage stores and worth the money. Tuck your shirt or pants over the top of it.

Nail Polish If you must take it with you, take only clear as it stops runs in pantyhose, and if it spills, it won't be such a disaster as red would be. Can be used to repair glasses in a pinch; if your lenses fall out of the frames, apply to the outside of lens and along the edge of the frame to keep the lens in place.

Nail Polish Remover Pads If you must take polish, take these new handy remover pads. In packages of ten, they will not break open like polish tends to do, nor leak.

Needlepoint Crafts to keep you busy while waiting for delayed flights, trains or buses.

Organizers to either hang in your garment bag or fold over in your suitcase. They save time when unpacking and are handy for changing, when the bathroom is down the hall. These can be small for jewelry or large for toiletries, shirts, socks, or anything.

Passport & Passport Wallet to keep all your documents together. Keep your passport, inoculations certificate, airline tickets, copy of your itinerary including names of hotels (in case you're separated from your group or travel companion), medic alert card, any large-size money, travelers checks, etc., together.

Perfume Samples that come in small vials are best for traveling, rather than a huge bottle of perfume. Also, perfume samples found in magazines work well.

Pens and Pencils are always needed for notes. Take a few to keep track of expenses, give as gifts, etc. Keep within reach

Pad of Paper to record expenses and photographs you take and miscellaneous memos.

Plastic Bags Ziplock are best. Sandwich and quart size should accommodate almost all needs. Always take extra.

Playing Cards are very seldom given out as souvenirs any more so be sure to pack your own. Great to play while you're traveling. Take them with pictures of your home state and give them away before returning home.

Post Cards from Home to show new friends and give away.

Paperback Books and Magazines to read and then give away. Be sure to check the political scene and know what type of magazines are permitted into certain countries.

Plastic Sandals   as there is always the chance of germs in public showers, pools, baths. Europeans never leave home without these. You shouldn't either. Also good for the beach.

Portable Smoke Detector highly recommended for hotel rooms that may not have them installed. Good for long stays in a condominium in the event there is not one supplied.

Panic Pak makes a great bon voyage gift. Includes a sewing kit, bobby pins, rubber bands, anything you may need along the way.

Pins/Paper Clips are very handy, from saving a torn seam to clipping your tickets together. Also super to mark a place in your guidebook or mark your visa for officials to find.

Pocket Calculator to keep track of expenses and converting foreign currency. A must. Solar powered are better than battery-run, as long as you have light. Keep it in your passport wallet for easy accessibility.

Radio small transistor radio is best. Take earphones to keep the noise down in small quarters.

Sarong/Pareo to use as a cover-up from hot glaring sun to air conditioning, which is too cold. Also to wear over shorts into museums, as a shawl, or for a picnic blanket.

Scarf large enough to cover your head as protection from the heat and cold but smaller than a sarong. Also wear while doing makeup to avoid messing your hair. Wear while dressing and undressing to keep makeup from your collars. (Less washing that way!)

Scotch/Masking/Duck Tape in small rolls or wrapped around a paper clip. Great for repairing emergency hems and securing bottle tops on tightly to avoid leakage. Also removes lint from clothing.

Sea Bands elasticized wrist bands that control nausea. They have changed the way travelers feel about cruises, airplanes, car and bus trips, etc!

Sewing Kit with extra needles, basic colors of thread, etc.

Sink Stopper for doing laundry in your room and avoid high cleaning costs. Many hotels do not provide them. Large rubber stopper should cover most drains completely.

Soap for bathing, washing, cleaning. Some travelers are allergic to the soaps provided in foreign accommodations if it's even supplied. Take along your own soap bars and slip into plastic bags, or take a biodegradable liquid soap that's multi-purpose and easy to use for laundry as well.

Shower Cap is almost never found in a hotel room or cabin these days, so come prepared. In a pinch, wrap a towel or scarf round your head.

Shoe Laces to fit all your shoes. Before you leave home, replace old laces in your traveling shoes but just in case, take spare pair along. May also be used in place of string.

Stain Remover when there's no time to do laundry.

Stereo Cassette Player in a compact size. Great for learning a foreign language while en route. Or before leaving home, tape some of your favorite operas, musicals, radio stations, etc. Consider purchasing a player with radio and record the native sounds or tour information of your trip.

String Bag hand crocheted cotton with handles long enough for carrying over your shoulder. Rolls into a ball for ease in packing. Great for grocery shopping.

Straws prevent exposure to various bacteria, especially on bottles.

Stretch Cords can't be beat for keeping purchases made along the way together.

Sticky Address Labels to label your camera and all important equipment. (Use your business address only.) Take extras with you in case you purchase new items along the way.

Sunscreen check the SPF and don't forget waterproof sunscreen is fantastic for a beach holiday.

Sunglasses not only for hot weather holidays, as sun is also prevalent in cold climates, and especially harsh around the snow. Attaching string around the ends to enable you to "hang" your glasses around your neck instead of putting them down is recommended to avoid losing them.

Swiss Army Knife don't leave home without one! Packed in your checked luggage only. This magical item is a lifesaver. Be sure to purchase one with many attachments; some of the most essential are: scissors, tweezers, corkscrew, bottle opener, and knife to cut everything, including your grapefruit.

Tape Measure for shopping.

Tip Table , the size of a credit card, which has invaluable information for tipping everyone from waiters to doormen.

Toiletries if you are particular about yours, make sure you take along enough to last the entire trip plus, if you have room, one week in case you extend. If you are more adventurous, most items can be purchased anywhere, depending on how exotic your trip is. The more exotic, the more you need to take. Trial size toothpaste is an easy item to take and toss when empty.

Toilet Paper always a necessity, even when going to the zoo in your own home town. Take out the cardboard roll and *squish* to save space. Pack a small amount in a Ziplock bag in your purse or pack. Travel-sized Kleenex will also suffice.

Toilet Seat Covers are not to be found in many foreign countries. If you are accustomed to them, take your own supply.

Trash Bags large enough to use for an impromptu rain poncho if necessary. Help to keep the wrinkles down in your luggage as well. Also can be used to sit on damp benches.

Travel Alarm Clock battery operated. Packs flat with little space. An illuminated dial makes it easy to read the time in unfamiliar rooms so you won't knock everything off the night stand. Make sure you know how to use it before leaving home

Travel Medical Kit in the event of an emergency or just to take care of small incidents along the way.

Temporary Filling for dental purposes. In case a filling falls out on holiday and you don't want to go to an unfamiliar dentist or there isn't one for hundreds of miles. Or you can try melted wax in an emergency. Consult your dentist for further information.

Travel Diary to record your holiday. It's very easy to forget the exciting things that happened when you're constantly moving. Quite fun to look back on in years to come. Also to use as a reference for friends who are going to the same places.

Washcloth for day-to-day needs. When wet, place in a plastic bag for quick cleanups from picnics. Also can be used, rinsed in warm water, wrung out, and wiped over wrinkles to hang out wrinkles in clothes.

Watch with an alarm if you have one and know how to use it. Be sure to change the batteries before you leave, if necessary. Waterproof watches are a good idea for beach holidays. And you can set the alarm while traveling, for example on the plane, to awaken you before your destination.

Water Purifier for extended trips. Saves money on bottled water.

Umbrella a small collapsible one. Great for rainy days as well as the intense rays of the sun.

Video Camera, including extra tapes, adapter, batteries.